PART ONE   **Horn in F**

FIRST DIVISION BAND COURSE

FIRST DIVISION BAND METHOD

by FRED WEBER

HELLO, Band Students:

You are about to start an activity that should bring you much pleasure, fun, and happiness. As with all worthwhile things, a reasonable amount of effort and work, together with daily practice, will be necessary for success. We have tried in every way possible to make the work in this book enjoyable and challenging to you. At the same time it provides for the fine background in musical fundamentals so necessary to become a good player. Your success will depend to a large degree on the effort you put forth. Remember: The better player you become, the more fun you will have.

Best wishes in your new undertaking.

Sincerely yours,

Fred Web

Author, First Division Band Method

Published for

Conductor & Piano Accompaniment	E♭ Baritone Saxophone
Flute	B♭ Trumpet
B♭ Clarinet	Horn in F
E♭ Alto Clarinet	Trombone
B♭ Bass Clarinet	Baritone B.C.
Oboe	Baritone T.C.
Bassoon	Tuba
E♭ Alto Saxophone	Drums
B♭ Tenor Saxophone	Bells

ELEMENTARY FINGERING CHART

How To Read The Chart

❚ - means lever DOWN

◖ - means lever UP

When two notes are given together on the chart (F♯ and G♭), they sound the same and, of course, are played with the same fingering.

In order to make the fingering chart as easy to understand as possible, only those fingerings necessary in the elementary phase of French Horn playing are given.

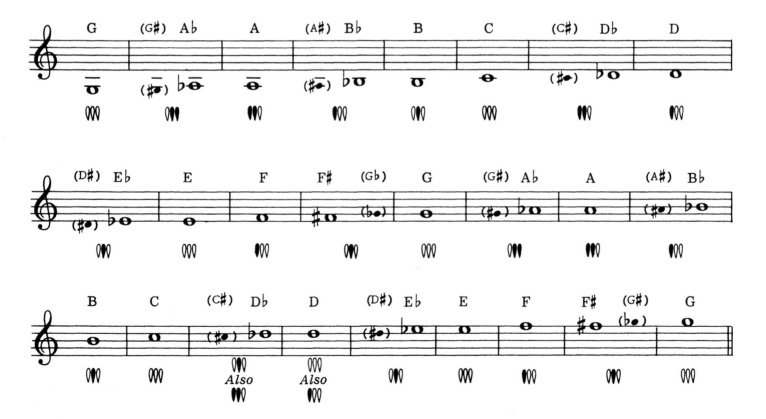

To The Student:

This Method Book is basic text for the FIRST DIVISION BAND COURSE series. To get the most enjoyment from your band activities and to ensure a good mastery of musical fundamentals, what you learn in the Method Book should be applied to the playing of solos, ensembles, and full band pieces as your skill increases.

On various pages in this Method Book, supplementary material is suggested, specially written for your playing ability. It is strongly recommended that these numbers be prepared as the various pages are reached.

MATERIAL CORRELATED WITH THE FIRST DIVISION BAND METHOD, PART ONE:

Solos for Horn in F

TIME FOR SOLOS!, BOOK ONE

Correlated to
Method pages:

THE HUNTSMAN . . . . .Leonard B. Smith 15
ed. by Philip Farkas
TIGER EYE . . . . .Leonard B. Smith 15
OUR FAVORITE . . . . .Leonard B. Smith 20
ed. by Philip Farkas
MOUNTAIN SHADOWS . . . . .Leonard B. Smith 20
COUNT DOWN . . . . .Leonard B. Smith 24
ed. by Philip Farkas
INDIGO . . . . .Leonard B. Smith 24
(Some solos may also be available separately)

Technic
FUN WITH
FUNDAMENTALS . . . . .Bill Laas & Fred Weber . . . . Part 1 & 2

Concert Band Books
OUR FIRST CONCERT ▪ AWAY WE GO ▪ PLAY AWAY ▪ CENTER STAGE

Concert Band Pieces
FDL9901 BIG BASS BOOGIE . . . . .James D. Ployhar
FDL9902 MEXICANA . . . . arr. Frank Erickson
FDL9903 OVERTURE FOR YOUTH . . . . Eric Osterling
FDL9904 SOMEBODY'S KNOCKING AT YOUR DOOR. . . arr. James D. Ployhar
FDL9905 WILLIAM TELL (Featuring the Trumpet Section) . . . . . Michael Story
FDL9906 KRAZY KLOCK II . . . . .James D. Ployhar

Know Your Instrument

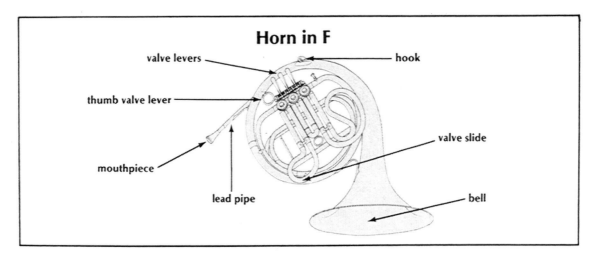

Horn in F

valve levers — hook

thumb valve lever —

valve slide

mouthpiece

lead pipe

bell

How To Assemble Your Instrument:

1. Hold the instrument with your LEFT HAND by grasping the tubing near the valves. Rest the BELL near your RIGHT KNEE.

2. With your right hand, place the MOUTHPIECE into the MOUTHPIECE STEM and turn slightly to the right. DO NOT TURN TOO TIGHTLY!

How To Hold Your Instrument:

1. Rest the bottom edge of the BELL on your right leg. Find a spot where the bell feels firm and secure.

2. Place the little finger of your LEFT HAND in the hook.

3. Place your left thumb under the lead pipe on the thumb hook or thumb valve lever.

4. Place the fleshy part of your first three fingers squarely on the valve levers.

5. Keep your left arm relaxed.

6. Your RIGHT HAND is held as if you were about to shake hands.

7. Your right thumb is closed against the forefinger. The result is a slightly cupped hand with the thumb up.

8. Your hand then is placed in the BELL with the backs of the fingers against the bell. Your thumb should be pointing up in the direction of the main bell brace.

9. Keep at least two inches between the ball of your hand and the bell, with a slightly cupped hand.

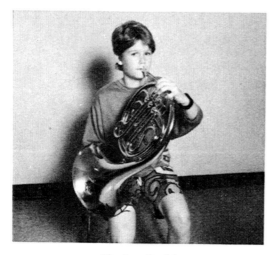

Playing Position

Right Hand Position in Bell

These photos show you the proper way to hold the horn.

GETTING STARTED

On the Horn in F we can get several different tones without any valves - using different LIP positions.

<u>FIRST</u> <u>DO</u> <u>THIS</u> - Play any open tone (<u>no</u> <u>levers</u> <u>down</u>). Hold it as long as <u>comfortable</u> and try to make the tone as <u>clear</u> and <u>steady</u> as possible. Be sure the air goes through the horn in a steady stream.

The tone you play will probably be one of THREE tones. We will call them "HIGH", "MIDDLE", and "LOW". Your teacher will tell you which one you are playing

———————————— HIGH

———————————— MIDDLE

———————————— LOW

High tones are easier for some beginners while others find the low tones easier to play.

The note below is the LOW tone from above.

The note below is the MIDDLE tone from above.

The note below is the HIGH tone from above.

If you have the correct notes above, the sound of playing the three tones, in order, is the same as do, mi, sol.

<u>PRACTICE</u> <u>THE</u> <u>NOTES</u> <u>ABOVE</u> until you can play them with a steady and pleasant sounding tone.

<u>WHEN</u> <u>YOU</u> <u>CAN</u> <u>PLAY</u> <u>THE</u> <u>NOTES</u> <u>ABOVE</u> try playing the notes below, using the proper levers when necessary. *MEMORIZE.*

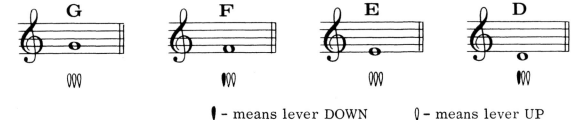

❙ - means lever DOWN   ❪ - means lever UP

<u>PLAY</u> <u>THE</u> <u>LINE</u> <u>BELOW</u>. Hold each tone as long as comfortable, and be sure it sounds pretty and is clear and steady.

Sound ——➤ do mi sol mi do

<u>NOTE:</u> Many young Horn players use the do, mi, sol, pattern above before starting each line, to help them find the correct starting tone.

F.D.L.13

Reading Music

You should know these things before we start to play.

STAFF	CLEF SIGN (Treble)	BAR	MEASURE	DOUBLE BAR
5 lines and 4 spaces		Divides the staff into measures	Space between two bars	Marks the end of a section

WHOLE NOTE — Play 4 Counts

WHOLE REST — Rest 4 Counts

TIME SIGNATURE — 4 Counts in each measure

Items in these ovals are NEW, or used for the first time.

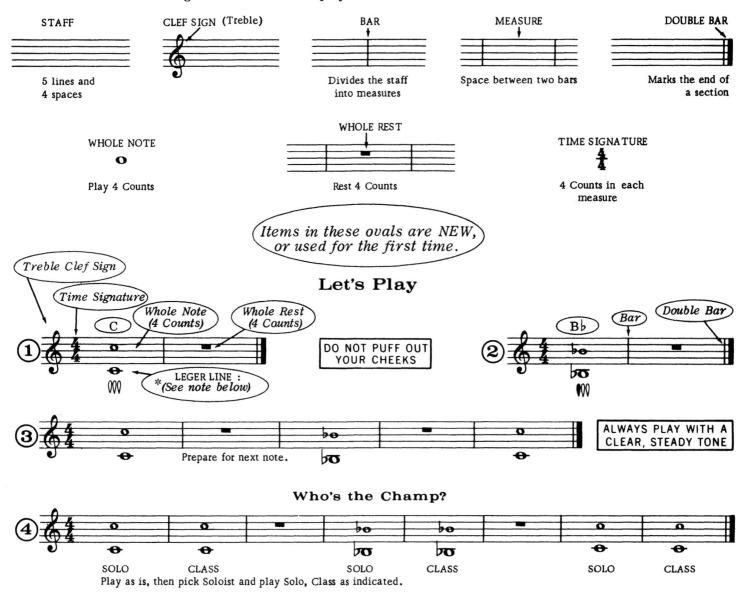

Let's Play

DO NOT PUFF OUT YOUR CHEEKS

ALWAYS PLAY WITH A CLEAR, STEADY TONE

Prepare for next note.

Who's the Champ?

SOLO CLASS SOLO CLASS SOLO CLASS
Play as is, then pick Soloist and play Solo, Class as indicated.

In the beginning, High Notes are easier for some players. Those having trouble with the LOW notes may play the smaller (or cued) notes in the High Octave for the first few pages. If you play the High notes, you should be working on the LOW tones so you can play them as soon as possible.

PROPER PLAYING POSITION IS MOST IMPORTANT

MAKE EACH NOTE AS PRETTY AND PLEASANT AS POSSIBLE

Name the notes before you play.

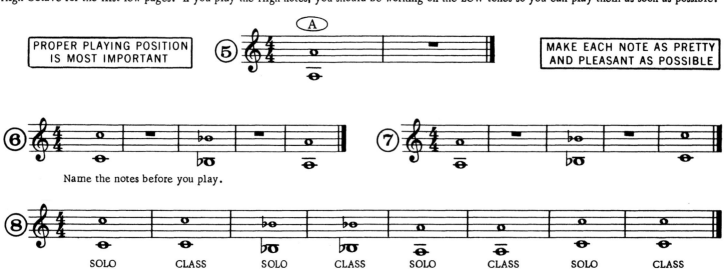

SOLO CLASS SOLO CLASS SOLO CLASS SOLO CLASS

* LEGER LINES: Many times we use notes that go above or below the staff. We provide for these notes by adding short lines called Leger Lines. By placing notes on these lines or the spaces between them, we are able to go above or below the staff.

For the first few pages name and finger the notes before you play each line.

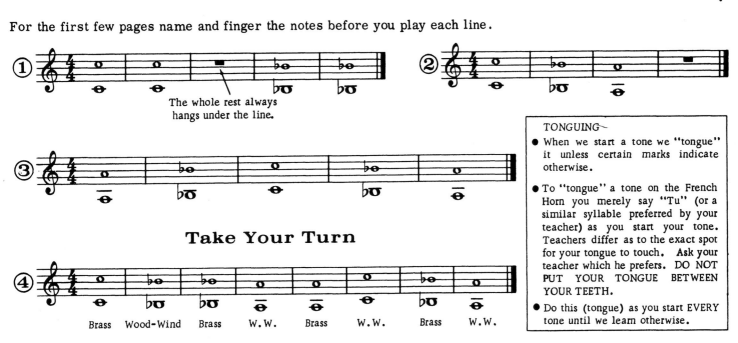

The whole rest always hangs under the line.

TONGUING~
- When we start a tone we "tongue" it unless certain marks indicate otherwise.
- To "tongue" a tone on the French Horn you merely say "Tu" (or a similar syllable preferred by your teacher) as you start your tone. Teachers differ as to the exact spot for your tongue to touch. Ask your teacher which he prefers. DO NOT PUT YOUR TONGUE BETWEEN YOUR TEETH.
- Do this (tongue) as you start EVERY tone until we learn otherwise.

Take Your Turn

Brass   Wood-Wind   Brass   W.W.   Brass   W.W.   Brass   W.W.

Quarter Notes and Rests

Quarter Note (1 Count)
Quarter Rest (1 Count)
*Also B♭ *See note below.*

TONGUE EVERY NOTE

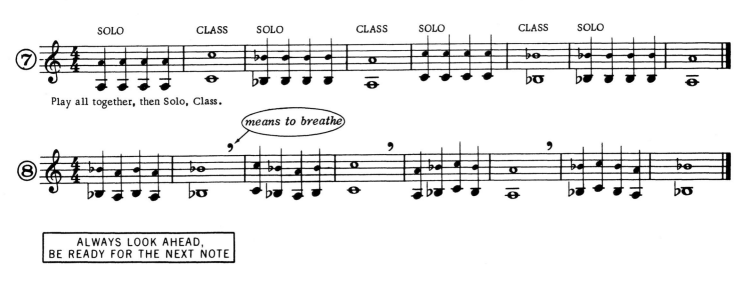

In this book there will be many times when two lines can be played together. This will be indicated by a broken vertical line joining them. Always learn each line separately first. The class should then be divided and the lines played together.

SOLO   CLASS   SOLO   CLASS   SOLO   CLASS   SOLO

Play all together, then Solo, Class.

means to breathe

ALWAYS LOOK AHEAD,
BE READY FOR THE NEXT NOTE

French Horn Extras

Ⓓ Ⓔ♭ Ⓕ

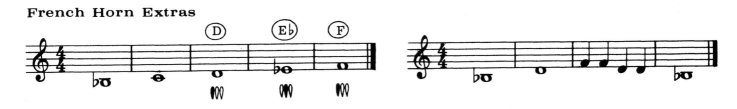

* A Flat or Sharp remains in effect throughout the entire measure.

8

A very important story

As a beginner the most important thing is the development of careful playing habits. Always be sure of these things:

1. Proper position - lips, hands, fingers, posture, etc.

2. Always get a pretty and pleasant tone with no wavers.
3. Tongue all notes correctly.
4. Blow plenty of AIR through the horn.
5. Always LISTEN carefully.

* See Note below ⑥ on Page 7.

Mary's Little Lamb

Half Notes and Rests

Count ① ② ③ ④ Half Rest always sets on top of the line.

Count ① ② ③ ④

ALWAYS LOOK AHEAD

Holiday In Paris (Duet)

* See Note below ⑥ on Page 7.

French Horn Extra

* HARMONY - Two or more Tones played at the same time that have a pleasing sound.

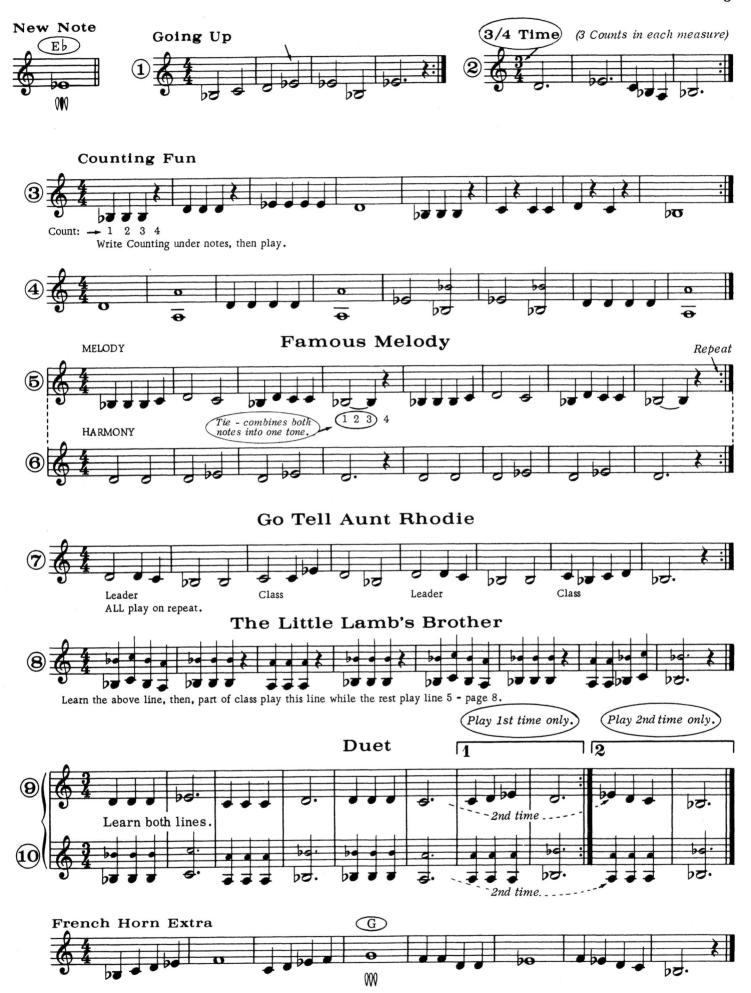

New Note Eb

Going Up ①

3/4 Time (3 Counts in each measure) ②

Counting Fun ③

Count: → 1 2 3 4
Write Counting under notes, then play.

④

Famous Melody

MELODY ⑤ *Repeat*

HARMONY ⑥

Tie - combines both notes into one tone. 1 2 3 4

Go Tell Aunt Rhodie ⑦

Leader Class Leader Class
ALL play on repeat.

The Little Lamb's Brother ⑧

Learn the above line, then, part of class play this line while the rest play line 5 - page 8.

Play 1st time only. Play 2nd time only.

Duet 1 2

⑨ Learn both lines. ~2nd time~

⑩ ~2nd time~

French Horn Extra G

Solo Boy

Solo   Class   Solo   Class

Counting Fun

New Notes

ALWAYS PLAY WITH A CLEAR, STEADY TONE

New Note

Common Time - C
Same as 4/4

Here's That Tune Again

The Two Tune Duet

Learn each line separately, then divide class and play together.

1 2 3   1 2 3
Count

Put the following on the Staff:

Whole Note	Flat	Quarter Note	A Time Signature	Quarter Rest	Half Note	Half Rest	Tie Two Notes

Comparing C and ¢ Time

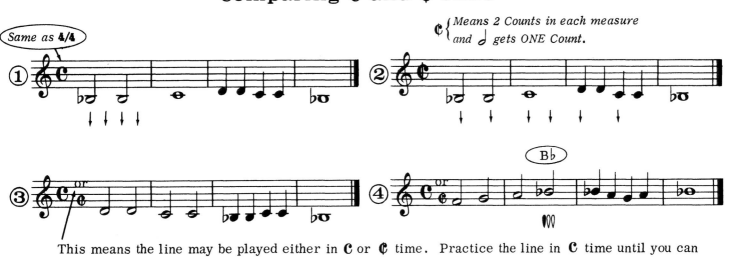

This means the line may be played either in C or ¢ time. Practice the line in C time until you can play it well, then play the notes at the same speed but TAP in ¢ time. The notes will sound the same, only the TAPPING will be different.

Write counting below lines ⑦ and ⑧.

Count RESTS carefully. Clap Rhythms.

Work out carefully in 4/4 time, then try in ¢ time.

* The flats (or sharps) at the beginning of a piece are called the "Key Signature". A flat in the key signature means that this note is flatted throughout the entire piece. When there is one flat in the key signature it is always Bb. When there are two, they are always Bb and Eb. We use the key signature so it won't be necessary to use a flat (or sharp) before each note.

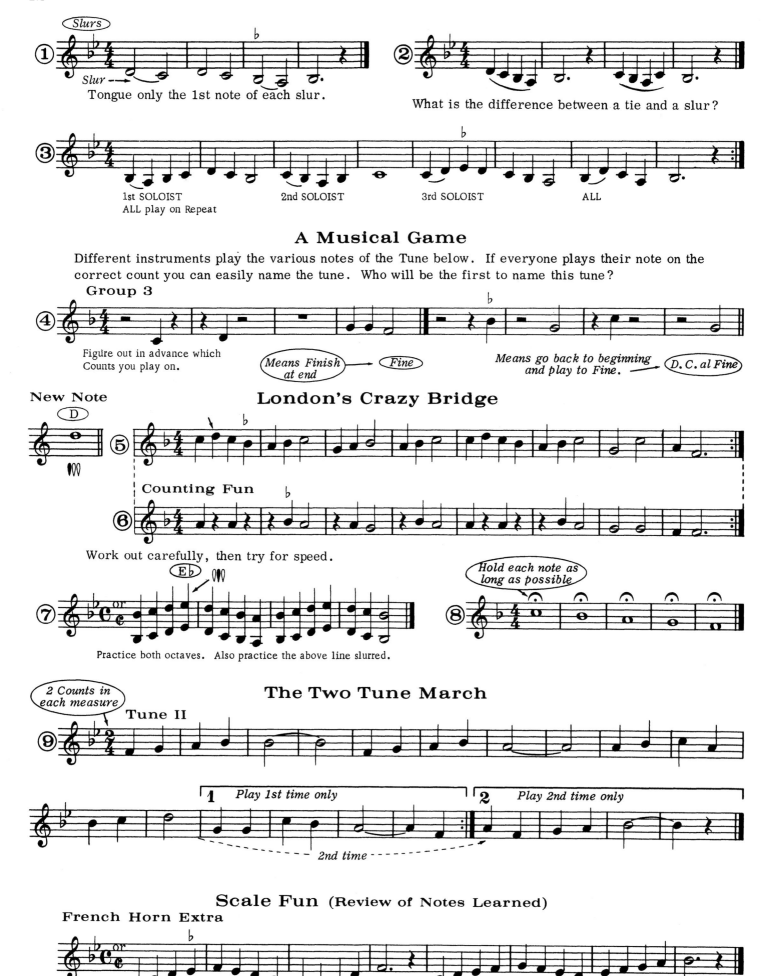

① *Slurs*

Slur → Tongue only the 1st note of each slur.

② What is the difference between a tie and a slur?

③ 1st SOLOIST 2nd SOLOIST 3rd SOLOIST ALL
ALL play on Repeat

A Musical Game

Different instruments play the various notes of the Tune below. If everyone plays their note on the correct count you can easily name the tune. Who will be the first to name this tune?

Group 3

④ Figure out in advance which Counts you play on.

Means Finish at end → *Fine*

Means go back to beginning and play to Fine. → *D. C. al Fine*

New Note

London's Crazy Bridge

⑤

Counting Fun

⑥

Work out carefully, then try for speed.

Hold each note as long as possible

⑦ *or* Practice both octaves. Also practice the above line slurred.

⑧

The Two Tune March

2 Counts in each measure — Tune II

⑨

1 *Play 1st time only*   *2* *Play 2nd time only*

- - - 2nd time - - -

Scale Fun (Review of Notes Learned)

French Horn Extra

or

Work out carefully, then try for speed.

OUR FIRST SOLO

I Love You Truly

You are now ready to play the first two solos from the book TIME FOR SOLOS! BOOK ONE. They were specially written for your playing ability at this time. It will be fun to get this book for your instrument and learn these solos.

Also play using half notes on each tone. Play using 4 quarter notes on each tone. Do the same playing backwards.   (Up the scale, playing last note first.)

E Flat - E♭

(Also practice slurring each measure.)

E Natural - E♮
(Just plain E)

Pick-up Notes - Why?

Marine's March

Count: 4/4 → 3 4 1 etc.
¢ → 2 + 1 etc.

Fine
(Finish)

D.C. al Fine
(Back to beginning)

Peter The Pumpkin Eater Fantasy

Learn each line separately as Counting Fun, then a divided class should play lines together.

Jet Pilot March

MELODY

mf → *moderately loud*

BAND ACCOMP.

1 *Cancels the Flat in the Key Signature*

2

You are now ready to play the first concert from your first full band book called OUR FIRST CONCERT. It was written by some of the country's finest band composers and arrangers.

Slurs

Featuring Mr. Clarinet

The Mouse And The Clock

What's My Name?

Play each line separately as a Counting Study.

When the two lines are played together by a divided class, we have a familiar melody.

Hear That German Band

p → *soft*

repeat preceding measure

The Carnival Of Venice

f → *loud*

You are now ready to play the third and fourth solos from the book TIME FOR SOLOS! BOOK ONE. We know you will like playing them.

Three ways to count Old MacDonald

There's A Hole In The Bucket

Billy Boy

This Old Man

Round And Round We Go

Crazy Counting

Skip To M' Lou

Apply these patterns to each note of the scale above.

The Blue Tail Fly

MELODY

mf

BAND ACCOMP.

p

Birthday Greetings

BAND ACCOMP. PART ONLY

means to Pause

Three Tunes

(Clapping Song)

These 3 melodies may be played separately,
or together with the Band Accompaniment.

Accent marks

f

(Carnival Of Venice)

f

(Oh, Where! Oh, Where!)

f

Band Accomp. for all 3 melodies above.

mf

The fifth and sixth solos of TIME FOR SOLOS! BOOK ONE should be learned at this time. These solos can be used for Solo Festival participation.

Play Tunes

The pieces on this page are for extra practice and recreation. You may try them whenever you feel you are able to play them. All instruments may play together except E♭ Mellophone, Horn in F, Oboe, and Tenor Saxophone.

Home On The Range

We Wish You A Merry Christmas

I'm Called Little Buttercup

When The Saints Go Marching In

Red River Valley

Taps

Review and Rating (For <u>like</u> instruments only)

Notes

Counting

Time Signature

Key Signature

Slurring

Tone
Slowly
Breathe
Very smooth and Songlike

Etude

8 – Play the B♭ Scale up and down from Memory, slowly, 1 count on each note.

9 – Solo

10 – Ensembles

(Perfect is 10)	Points	(Perfect is 10)	Points
1 – Notes		6 – Tone	
2 – Counting		7 – Etude	
3 – Time Signatures		8 – Scale	
4 – Key Signatures		9 – SOLO	
5 – Slurring		10 – ENSEMBLES	
TOTAL POINTS ——————			

The teacher may use this Review and Rating page as he or she chooses. Each line may be played individually and rated by the teacher, or the page can be used as a review lesson. It may be the basis for awarding a certificate or diploma, or it may be used as a final rating for a report card or as a final record of accomplishment on completion of this book. Every item is rated on the basis of 10 possible points. The solo and ensemble categories should be rated on how well you performed any solos or ensembles during the year.

BAND CONCERT
Away We Go

When there are two or more Horn players, divide the notes below.
Half play TOP notes, and half the BOTTOM.

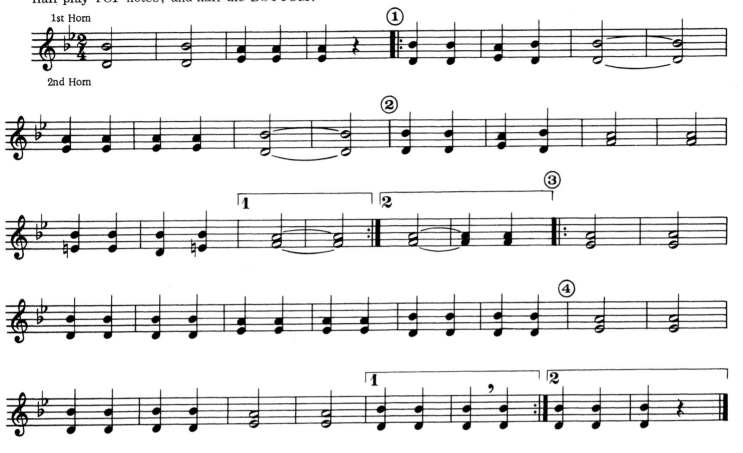

Two Famous Waltz Melodies

Musical Signs and Terms

(See page 6 for 1st elements of music)

Notes	and		Rests		Time Signatures

o — Whole —   **4/4** — 4 beats in each measure. / each ♩ note gets one beat.

♩ — Half —   **C** — Common Time - same as **4/4**

♩. — Dotted Half —   **3/4** — 3 beats in each measure. / each ♩ note gets one beat.

♩ — Quarter — ❟   **2/4** — 2 beats in each measure. / each ♩ note gets one beat.

♪ — Eighth — ❞   **¢** — 2 beats in each measure. / each ♩ note gets one beat.

♭ — Flat - Lowers a tone a ½ step.

♯ — Sharp - Raises a tone a ½ step.

♮ — Natural - Indicates that the note is not to be sharped or flatted. It cancels the effect of a sharp or flat.

❜ — Breath Mark

Repeat Dots - Repeat entire section.

1st and 2nd endings. Play 1st ending the first time then repeat strain and play 2nd ending.

o ♩ Tie - Combines two or more tones.

Chord - A combination of different tones that is pleasant to the ear.

Fine - Finish - The end.

D.C. al Fine - Go back to the beginning and play until you come to Fine.

Scale - A series of notes that follow a definite pattern of half steps and whole steps.

·/· - Repeat the preceding measure.

Waltz - A type of dance in **3/4** time.

Accompaniment - A part that supports the melody but is subordinate to it.

Home Practice Record

WEEK	MON.	TUES.	WED.	THURS.	FRI.	SAT.	PARENT'S SIGNATURE	WEEK	MON.	TUES.	WED.	THURS.	FRI.	SAT.	PARENT'S SIGNATURE
1								19							
2								20							
3								21							
4								22							
5								23							
6								24							
7								25							
8								26							
9								27							
10								28							
11								29							
12								30							
13								31							
14								32							
15								33							
16								34							
17								35							
18								36							